The Lost Art
Secrets of Disciple-Making

by
Dan Vis

All Scripture quotations are from the
King James Version of the Bible
Emphasis supplied unless otherwise indicated.

ISBN: 978-1-958155-03-5

Published by FAST Missions
111 2nd Street
Kathryn, ND 58049

Additional copies of this book are available by
visiting us at WWW.FAST.ST

Dedication

This book is dedicated to my precious wife, who has been my love and constant companion through all our years together. Thank you!

Table of Contents

The Lost Art
Preface

Usually, when someone writes their memoirs, they are famous, or at least have something remarkable about their life that makes people want to read their story. That's not the case here. While I've had the privilege to travel the world and speak in hundreds of venues to thousands of people—I'm far from famous. And my life story is not really all that remarkable.

But it does hint at a remarkable truth: that God can reach anyone, anywhere, with a revelation of Himself. He reached out to me, when my young life, so filled with promise, had completely spiraled out of control—and I was rushing toward one of three almost certain outcomes: drug overdose, incarceration, or a psychotic break with reality.

But God did more than just reveal Himself. He enrolled me in my own private Anti-Seminary.

It was a school built on personal study, prayer and Bible memorization. A school that enabled me to find surprising answers to questions that had perplexed me for years—right where I was. To find truth in all the wrong places. And I'm still enrolled in that school today.

It's not that I'm opposed to formal theological training. Not at all! I would have loved to enter those ivory towers and sit at the feet of men who had spent their whole lives studying about God. But those opportunities never quite seemed to present themselves to me. And I ended up taking a far less cultivated path, and stumbled my way into the secret place of the Most High. I discovered how to learn directly from Him.

This is the story of a young man, who made a shocking discovery—while just barely out of his teens. A discovery that soon unlocked answers to some of mankind's greatest mysteries. Mysteries that puzzle thousands, still today. And ultimately, that led to the birth of a ministry that is equipping thousands around the world with tools and training they can use to enroll in their own anti-seminaries.

If you've ever wanted to find out the truth about God for yourself, or maybe just wanted to learn to draw a bit closer to Him—this book is for you. Sit back and enjoy the story.

The Example of Jesus
Chapter 1

In recent years, there has been a growing awareness that the Great Commission is not just about baptizing new believers. More and more, church leaders are beginning to understand that the work of "making disciples" also involves teaching our members the basic principles of the Christian life, and helping them grow toward spiritual maturity. And churches everywhere are attempting to make that shift toward a paradigm of disciple-making. Maybe you attend one of those churches...

But they are also discovering that it's not so easy to start making disciples. It has been a "lost art" for far too long, that few have any real idea even where to start. The information ahead can help.

If you have been asked to help lead a discipleship team, or just feel a personal burden to begin investing in the lives of a few friends, the next few days will help give you a solid biblical foundation for how to make disciples in your local church. Build your training ministry in harmony with these principles, and you will be sure to see lives changed. And you'll discover something else: helping others will deepen your own walk with God too!

Better still, it will draw you more fully into the heart of Christ. You see, making disciples was at the center of His ministry. Though He did many things while on earth, His primary focus was selecting twelve men, and then training them for leadership (Mark 3:14). They were taught how to memorize the Word, pray, deal with pressures, preach, and more. Day by day, they grew in experience and spiritual power, as they walked with the Master.

At the end of His ministry, He commanded them to go out and do the same. "As my Father hath sent me, even so send I you" (John 20:21). "Go ye therefore and make disciples of all nations, baptizing them... and teaching them to observe all things whatsoever I have commanded you" (Matthew 28:19-20, margin). They were to win and train others, just as He had won and trained them.

And they did. The early church exploded with power as "the word of God increased; and the number of disciples multiplied in Jerusalem greatly" (Acts 6:7). Thousands were converted, and then taught "the apostles' doctrine" (Acts 2:41-42). Eventually, these believers scattered throughout the entire region "preaching the Word" to others (Acts 8:4). And everywhere God's Word went, it changed lives.

This continued throughout the New Testament, with Paul and other church leaders establishing training centers in strategic locations, where they could raise up and train more workers. Near the end of Paul's ministry, he urged Timothy (and us) to continue this very same work: "And the things that thou hast heard of me among many witnesses, the same commit thou to faithful men, who shall be able to teach others also." (II Timothy 2:2).

As long as the church kept its focus on equipping strong disciples and workers, it thrived. But when that focus began to blur, the church weakened. In other words, the success of the church was directly linked to its obedience to the Great Commission.

There is an urgent need today, to get back to this New Testament approach. Back to equipping leaders to reproduce. Back to empowering workers to multiply. Back to the example of Jesus. For it will only be by raising up a vast army from the men and women who comprise our church membership, that our world can ever be reached, and the work of God finished at last. No doubt this is the exact reason we're told "every church should be a training school for Christian workers" (CS, p 59). Because our only hope of ever reaching our world is to mobilize every member possible for ministry. Or to put it differently, we will have to use the method of the Great Commission if we are ever to finish the work of the Great Commission. We must learn to make disciples once again. That has to be our priority.

Are you ready to take up this ministry that Christ Himself began? If faithful, the rewards will be beyond our wildest expectations. God promises, "a little one shall become a thousand, and a small one a strong nation" (Isaiah 60:22). And again, "as the host of heaven cannot be numbered, neither the sand of the sea measured: so will I multiply [those] that minister unto me" (Jeremiah 33:22). It can happen!

But first, we have to rediscover this lost art. Get ready...

The Example of Jesus
Study Questions

How does the Great Commission involve more than just baptizing new believers?

How does the work of "making disciples" help us draw more fully into the heart of Christ?

What were the results when the New Testament church focused on growing strong disciples?

How important is it to recapture a vision for spiritual multiplication in our churches today?

Additional Notes:

Stages of Growth
Chapter 2

Once a person grasps the fact training believers as an integral part of the Great Commission, all sorts of questions come to mind. And principally, how exactly does one do it?

The Great Commission itself suggests an important first principle. According to Jesus, making disciples specifically involves teaching believers "to observe all things whatsoever I have commanded you" (Matthew 28:20). And those teachings, of course, are found in God's Word. In other words, our training needs to be fully Bible-centered.

The book of Acts confirms this was the focus of the New Testament church. There we read that the believers "went every where preaching the word." "The word of God grew and multiplied." "The word of the Lord was published throughout all the region." "Paul and Barnabas continued ... teaching and preaching the word." "So mightily grew the word of God and prevailed." (See Acts 8:4, Acts 12:24, Acts 13:49, Acts 15:35, Acts 19:20). Clearly, the Bible was at the heart of training in the New Testament, and to be effective in our training today, we must learn to do the same!

How We Grow

Founding our training on the Word makes sense—for it is Scripture that propels people through each stage of growth in the Christian life. Consider for a moment, the four stages of growth as outlined in the New Testament:

Stage 1. Unbelievers
Stage 2. Spiritual Babes
Stage 3. Disciples
Stage 4. Workers

A careful study of the Bible reveals how important Scripture is to each stage of growth. Unbelievers are "born again, not of corruptible seed, but of incorruptible, by the word of God" (I Peter 1:23). Spiritual Babes are told to "desire the sincere milk of the word, that [they] may grow thereby" (I Peter 2:2). Disciples are those who "continue in [Christ's] word" until they are made free from the grip of sin (John 8:31-32). And finally, Workers are those who "study to shew [themselves] approved unto God... rightly dividing the word of truth." (II Timothy 2:15).

The need at each stage, is essentially a deeper experience in the Word.

The Individual's Responsibility

To put it differently, there are specific things an individual must do at each stage to grow. Think of it as a roadmap every believer must pass through if they are to grow to full maturity. Steps on an important journey.

These steps can be seen clearly in Paul's first letter to the Thessalonians. There, he reminds them how they first heard the Word, through Paul's preaching "in power" (vs 1:5). Second, they received the word "with joy of the Holy Ghost" (vs 6).

Third they began living the word, becoming "ensamples to all that believe" (vs 7). And finally, they shared the word, proclaiming it "in every place" (vs 8).

This chart captures the idea:

Stage 1. Unbelievers   *Must*   *Hear the Word*
Stage 2. Spiritual Babes Must   *Receive the Word*
Stage 3. Disciples   *Must*   *Live the Word*
Stage 4. Workers   *Must*   *Share the Word*

Note that evangelism and training are two separate things. While evangelism helps unbelievers to become Christians, training helps them grow from spiritual babe, to disciple, to worker. An effective training program thus, is one that provides all the information and skills necessary to deepen their experience in God's Word. It helps them learn to take it in, live it out, and then pass it on.

Clearly, the Bible needs to be central in any training curriculum!

The Church's Responsibility

To help people progress through these various stages, the church too has specific responsibilities it must fulfil. Paul, for example, can be seen ministering to individuals at all four stages of growth throughout the book of Acts. In chapter 14, for example, we find him involved with evangelism at Derbe when he "preached the gospel to that city, and... taught many" (vs 21). Then, he "returned again" to meet with existing believers, and "confirm" or establish them in the faith (vs 22). He is next seen exhorting them to "continue in the faith" as mature disciples, regardless of hardship or cost (vs 22). And finally, we see him setting apart leaders "in every church" having "commended them to the Lord" (vs 23)—thus equipping them for service.

Notice the stages again:

Stage 1. The Church   Must   Evangelize Unbelievers
Stage 2. The Church   Must   Establish Spiritual Babes
Stage 3. The Church   Must   Exhort Disciples
Stage 4. The Church   Must   Equip Workers

Essentially, these tasks revolve around sharing the right Bible truths at the right time. Unbelievers need to hear the great truths of the cross, for "the gospel of Christ ... is the power of God unto salvation" (Romans 1:16). Spiritual babes must be rooted in the basics of joyous Christian living, by feeding them "with milk, and not with meat" (I Corinthians 3:1-2). But disciples, at some point, must be challenged with the "tougher" truths of Scripture if they are ever to become "strong" in the Word (I John 2:14). And finally, workers must be inspired with a biblical "vision" for their life, that enables them to "look on the fields" and see "they are white already to harvest" (John 4:35).

Again we see, God's Word must stay at the center of our training. That Scripture is able to "thoroughly furnish" our members for service, through each of these critical stages (II Timothy 3:16-17).

Shortcuts Short-Circuit

Sometimes however, we get in trouble by teaching these things out of order. Soul-winning training, for example, often yields meager results because we fail to take into account these stages of growth. We may offer an afternoon workshop on how to give personal Bible studies—but only a handful come out. Why? Many of our members are spiritual babes, still learning to take in the Word regularly. Or they may be weak in discipleship, struggling to build the Word into key areas of their life. Deep down, they know they are not ready to become a Bible worker! These programs would be far more effective if we would first give the legitimate spiritual needs of these members the attention they deserve, without skipping steps, and thus help bring them to the point they are ready to reach out.

In laboring where there are already some in the faith, the minister should at first seek not so much to convert unbelievers, as to train the church members for acceptable co-operation. Christian Service, p. 70

The New Testament, in contrast, shows what happens when there is process in place to help believers to pass through these stages of growth. Those who joined these churches were taught how to internalize Scripture effectively, how to apply it practically to their life, and how to pass it on to others consistently. That is, they were taught how to multiply. And the Gospel spread with amazing speed. Soon Christians were rejoicing that the Gospel was bringing "forth fruit" in "all the world" (Colossians 1:6). And unbelievers were lamenting that this new sect had "turned the world upside down" (Acts 17:6).

It can happen again today. But we must get back to the Bible. Our churches must once again become effective training centers. And we must never forget, that shortcuts short-circuit the plan.

Tomorrow we look at how to train...

Stages of Growth
Discussion Questions

What are the four stages of spiritual growth outlined in the New Testament?

-

-

-

-

What must the individual do to pass through these each stage of growth?

What is the church's responsibility to help people at each stage growth?

Explain why Scripture must always be central to the whole disciple-making process:

What happens when we attempt to take shortcuts in our training of members?

Additional Notes:

The Disciple's Wheel
Chapter 3

Today we are going to fine tune our thoughts about how to train disciples by asking a closely related question: what does a disciple actually look like? Because when the target is clear, it is much easier to aim at it! Here are just a few thoughts...

The Rim and the Hub

Suppose you were to symbolize a person's spiritual life as a tire, or wheel. The outside rim represents your outward life—all the things you say and do, the places you go, the people you interact with, and so on. It is where the rubber hits the road, so to speak. A true disciple longs to bring every aspect of their outward life into harmony with the will of Christ. Or to put it differently, they want a Spirit-filled daily life.

Now the power for that kind of life, of course, does not come from our outward circumstances, but rather from deep within: Christ in the heart. Revelation 3:20 depicts Jesus knocking at the door, longing to enter in. John 1:12 tells us that all who choose to receive Christ are given "power to become the sons of God". Paul says "Christ in you" is the great "hope of glory" for every believer (Colossians 1:27). This is true Christianity—Christ in the heart.

How does Christ come into the heart? It is primarily through the Word. New Testament believers were said to become "followers ... of the Lord, having received the word" (I Thessalonians 1:6). James instructs us to "receive with meekness the engrafted word, which is able to save your souls" (James 1:21). And Peter says we are "born again, not of corruptible seed, but of incorruptible, by the word of God, which liveth and abideth for ever" (I Peter 1:23). When we receive God's Word into the heart by faith, it has an energizing and transforming power. So our first priority must be teaching believers how to successfully internalize the Word.

This is one reason we prioritize memorization in all our training. Time and time again, we've seen memorization work as a powerful spark to trigger spiritual revitalization.

Four Spokes

But sometimes there is a disconnect between the heart where Christ dwells, and the daily life seen by the people around us. While Paul writes "as ye have therefore received Christ Jesus the Lord, so walk ye in him" (Colossians 2:6), and John writes "He that saith he abideth in him ought himself also so to walk" (I John 2:6)—the reality is, that doesn't always happen. Sometimes a little more structure needs to be put in place, for us to be fully "rooted and built up in him, and stablished in the faith" (Colossians 2:7). That is where training comes in.

To put it differently, we need to connect our inward power source to our outward daily life. The rim to the hub. So let's imagine now, four spokes going out like a compass from the hub at the center of the circle, and connecting to the outer rim of our daily life. These spokes, just like the spokes on a bicycle tire, are the means through which power is transferred from the hub to the rim. How grace flows from the heart into our daily life.

To help someone grow spiritually, we simply need to help them understand these spokes. Now in the Bible, you can find any number of spokes connected with personal discipleship. But in my study, I've found most of these can be grouped into four main areas: Bible study, Prayer, Obedience, and Witnessing.

Prayer and Bible study are the two primary means by which we connect with God. Think of these as the vertical spokes, with prayer ascending up to heaven, and Bible study rooted deep down into the Word. But rather than opposites, these spokes are actually, closely interconnected. Prayer should be tied to the revealed will and promises of God. And likewise, Bible study should always be done in an attitude of constant prayer. Together, through these two spokes, grace flows into the heart.

Obedience and Witnessing are the two primary means by which we interact with the world around us. One represents our life example, the other our life message. And again, these two are also closely interconnected. Living a godly life without sharing the power behind that life robs God of the glory He deserves. And sharing the message of the Gospel without a corresponding change in conduct certainly undermines our credibility of our witness. But when both are combined, these two spokes allow grace to flow out toward those we interact with.

Analogies

In some ways, the life of discipleship is like breathing. In and out. Through prayer and Bible study, grace flows into the life. And through our personal example, and spoken words, grace flows out to others.

For any of this to work, there needs to be a robust circulatory system. That is, prayer and Bible study are like the veins in our body, through which blood flows into the heart. And obedience and witnessing are like the arteries, through which blood is pumped out from the heart to the rest of the body. The whole spiritual life is designed to work as a system. It all works together.

To grow in discipleship, all four spokes are essential. One blocked artery or vein can be deadly. You can never stop breathing. If you want to lay a strong foundation in discipleship, keep your focus on these four components: Bible study, prayer, personal obedience, and witnessing.

Extending Beyond

Each of these spokes, of course, includes a broad range of specific skills. There are many methods and tools for Bible study, many important aspects of prayer, many keys to growing in obedience, and a whole checklist of evangelism skills. At FAST we offer whole courses on each of these spokes! And ultimately, you will want to make sure your training is as comprehensive and as balanced as possible too.

In time, as we grow in these skills, the spokes begin to extend beyond the outer rim of our daily life into various kinds of ministry. The more deeply and carefully we study the Bible, the more God can use us to teach Scripture to others. The more we learn to agonize in prayer, the more our life becomes one of intercession. The more we grow in obedience, the more effectively we can help others in their quest to overcome too. And the more focused we are on sharing our faith, the more evangelistic our lifework becomes. Ultimately, discipleship empowers believers to reach out in all these ways!

Training Teams

Understanding these spokes also suggests another important key to making disciples. And it is simply this: to build disciples effectively, you should seek to integrate each of these spokes into your training program itself. That is, your meetings should include real Bible study, earnest prayer, exhortation to obey, and ministry training.

It is interesting to note, many churches have groups that focus on one specific spoke or another. Study classes focused on Bible knowledge. Prayer bands that meet to pray. Support groups for helping members overcome in some area. And endless committees working to coordinate different ministries. These certainly have a place. But what I'm proposing is a new kind of group: a training team.

It's clear Jesus used teams to train His disciples (Mark 3:14), as did the Apostle Paul (Acts 20:4). And there are many benefits to using teams today. But it only works if you intentionally build all four spokes right into the structure of every team meeting. That is, aim for a rough balance between Bible study, time in prayer, accountability and goal setting, and practical ministry training. Let your team degenerate into mere Bible study only, or focus exclusively on any other spoke, and your team is unlikely to produce real workers. But consistently emphasize all four spokes equally, and you will have an ideal environment for growth.

Discipleship is not done in isolation, but in community. If we want to grow up "unto the measure of the stature of the fulness of Christ" we must remember this happens when "the whole body" is "fitly joined together and compacted by that which every joint supplieth" (Ephesians 4:13,16). Or to use simpler language, we must press together.

Tomorrow, we look at how to do training in a way that results in real change.

The Disciple's Wheel
Discussion Questions

What do the "rim" and "hub" of the disciples wheel represent? What is the relationship between them?

What are the four essential spokes of discipleship:

-

-

-

-

How are these components analogous to breathing? To the circulatory system?

Explain how these components should be built into the structure of a training team. What happens if your team meetings fail to include all four?

Why does discipleship happen best in community, rather than isolation?

Additional Notes:

The Training Recipe
Chapter 4

So far, we've covered a lot of ground. How the training process helps believers grow from spiritual babe to disciple, and then on to worker. We've also looked at some key areas of training: Our spiritual life starts with internalizing the Word. Then it grows as we lay a foundation of Bible study, prayer, personal obedience and witnessing. Ultimately it grows into a life of real ministry.

But we haven't yet talked much about how to train. How to help people start growing. That's our focus for today.

And actually, it's not a new problem. Spiritual babes existed in New Testament times just like they do today. Paul wrote that he was unable to speak to the Corinthians "as unto spiritual, but ... as unto babes in Christ" and had to feed them "with milk, and not with meat" for they were "not able to bear it" (I Corinthians 3:1-2). Even Jesus had to hold back things from His disciples at times, because they weren't ready to receive them (John 16:12). There is nothing wrong, of course, with a new Christian being a spiritual babe—the problem is staying a babe long after we have had ample time to grow up into a worker.

To get people moving down the process of growth once again, requires us to understand the New Testament's method of training.

A Recipe for Training

Recipes are important. If you want to have a consistent outcome in preparing some dish, it helps to record the essential ingredients and process you use to make it. The recipe allows you to replicate the desired outcome.

To have consistent success in our training efforts, it is important to have a recipe for training as well. And fortunately, the New Testament gives us just that recipe. In particular, the book of Hebrews gives us 4 key ingredients that are necessary to help a person transition from spiritual babe to disciple to worker. Watch carefully:

For when for the time ye ought to be teachers, ye have need that one teach you again which be the first principles of the oracles of God; and are become such as have need of milk, and not of strong meat. For every one that useth milk is unskilful in the word of righteousness: for he is a babe. But strong meat belongeth to them that are of full age, even those who by reason of use have their senses exercised to discern both good and evil. Hebrews 5:12-14

The Four Ingredients

The first thing we see in this passage is that spiritual babes need Scripture. They must be taught, once again, the "first principles" of the Bible. Even if they have heard it all before, we should go back over the basics of how we are to live our lives. The reason for this is simply to establish that the Bible is our rule of practice. And that we use it for everything we teach.

Second, they need skills. People get frustrated spiritually when information is not combined with the practical "know-how" needed to integrate that information into their daily life. This time through, we'll not only teach them the importance of Bible study, prayer, time management, and sharing our faith—we'll also show them how to do it. Step by step, we'll lay out the exact nuts and bolts of how to implement what the Bible says.

Next comes practice. Skills are not acquired the same way as information. To learn some fact we only need to hear it once or twice and then remember it. But skills are gained "by reason of use." They must be exercised. You don't learn to swim in a classroom. You have got to jump into some water—and practice! We don't put on muscles by watching a video on weight lifting. We have to get out and lift some barbells.

Finally, it just takes time for lives to change. Even with the best of training, no one grows to "full age" overnight! Individual skills often take weeks or months to learn. Which is why it is important to provide an extended period of training. A weekend conference can't do it. In many cases, to train an effective worker, you will have to stick by their side for as much as a year or longer—especially if they have a family, a career, or are busy with school. There's no way around it: training takes time.

Here then, are the basic ingredients of our New Testament training recipe: Scripture, skills, practice, and time. Or to put it differently:

Tell them why	*from the Scriptures*
Show them how	*in your own life*
Get them started	*with bite-size projects*
Keep them going	*by building commitment*

If you want to develop an effective training program, be sure each lesson includes a basic study, reviewing the Bible's teachings on that topic. Then give practical suggestions for how to build that principle into their life. There then needs to be weekly objectives to encourage implementation of those suggestions. And finally, you need to keep repeating those core concepts over and over again, until they finally sink in. It's a simple strategy, but it works.

A Practical Example

Suppose someone were to hear you quote a verse, and mention how they wished they could memorize Scripture too. What would you do?

If you follow the New Testament training formula, the steps are simple. "Hey that's great! Let's get together sometime and I'll be happy to show you just how to do it. It's easy". And you set a time.

At your first meeting, you start with a simple review of what the Bible teaches on the subject. You might say something like this: "Let's start by looking at a few verses from the Bible that show why memorization is important." Even though they may already be motivated, it's important they know that memorization is biblical. Scripture must be the foundation of everything you teach. *Tell them why.*

Then, you take a few moments explaining exactly how you memorize. Pull out your verse pack, and show them how you write out your cards, how you memorize them (phrase by phrase), and the importance of daily review, and of learning verses word-perfect. You don't have to cover everything right way—just enough to get them started. *Show them how.*

Next, you give them some small assignment to carry out. Choose a short, easy verse to help ensure they will have good initial success. Maybe Philippians 4:13 or Deuteronomy 6:6. You make sure they don't have any questions about what to do, and then set a target date for them to learn the verse. *Get them started.*

Last, plan another meeting to get with them and review how they do. Better yet, pick a regular time to meet each week for a while. Check up on their verses. Give them additional tips. Answer questions. Help them with difficulties. Set new goals. And continue each time to reinforce their commitment. *Keep them going.*

Bottom line: you stick with this process, until your friend has fully internalized this skill and no longer needs your external support. That's training.

Teaching Vs Training

A wise man once said telling isn't teaching. And it's true. To teach someone, you only have to communicate information. And make sure that information is received, understood, and remembered. Only then can you say you have truly taught someone.

But training involves even more. Teaching is the transference of information, but training is the transference of skills. And while that includes information, it also requires the nuts and bolts of how to implement that information. The person must practice the skill to master it. And they often need support and encouragement to stick with it.

Teaching may changes someone's beliefs, but training changes their life. To go from making informed converts to making mature disciples and ultimately skilled workers, we have to shift your focus from teaching to training. And to do that we must follow the recipe outlined above.

How will you ever find time to do all this training? Great question. We'll explore that next...

The Training Recipe
Worksheet

Why are recipes important? What is their purpose?

What four ingredients go into the New Testament "recipe" for training?

-
-
-
-

Why is it important to reteach the basics of the Christian life to members who may already be familiar with them?

Why is it important to combine information with practical, nuts and bolts skills?

Why is it impossible to learn skills without practice?

Why is it important to stick with someone for a while to ensure they learn a skill?

Summarize how you would train someone to memorize Scripture using this recipe:

Summarize the key differences between teaching and training:

Additional Notes:

The Time Problem
Chapter 5

It is difficult enough to find time to teach believers the basic doctrines of the Bible. But finding time to impart the basic skills of discipleship is even harder! Especially when we consider all the areas we need to cover, and the time it takes to really truly transfer skills. In fact, it may sound impossible—considering the busy lives people live today.

But there is no way around it. Crowded church schedules will definitely have to clear some space for disciple-making. But if we are serious about seeing our churches filled with workers once again, and finishing the work in this generation—we will have to get more serious about training. There's no other way!

Fortunately there are options. Some churches dedicate the mid-week prayer service to training, or choose some night of the week for small groups meeting in homes. Others organize an early session before church starts, or an afternoon session, after the worship service. But for many churches, there is another perfect slot for training.

Time for Training

Actually, God made room for it from the very beginning. At the end of creation week, God "blessed the seventh day, and sanctified it". That is, He "set it apart for sacred purposes". It was to be a day to meet with fellow believers and leave secular pursuits behind. It was intended to be an eternal safeguard, protecting busy people. See Genesis 2:2-3, Exodus 20:8-11, Isaiah 66:22-23, etc. The principle of the sabbath continues into New Testament times, as well, where we are told: "there remaineth therefore a keeping of sabbath to the people of God" (Hebrews 4:9, margin).

Notice Paul's use of the sabbath in the verses below:

And Paul, as his manner was, went in unto them, and three sabbath days reasoned with them out of the scriptures. Acts 17:2

And he reasoned in the synagogue every sabbath, and persuaded the Jews and the Greeks. Acts 18:4

After preaching in the synagogue at Antioch one sabbath, the Gentiles asked "that these words might be preached to them the next sabbath." Whether because these people worked during the week, or because he himself was busy working, Paul agreed to wait till then. "And the next sabbath day came almost the whole city together to hear the word of God" (Acts 13:42-44).

Similar conditions exist today. People are busy, and it is difficult to get them to come together outside our regular weekly worship service. So instead, offer training to them while they are already at church. Child care is readily available through the various children's divisions. And people are rested, awake and alert. It is the perfect time...

Back to School

I'm talking of course, about the weekly Bible study time most churches have prior to the worship service. In many churches, however, the study that happens here is little more than an open discussion that tends to degenerate into a battle of cliches and opinions. The quality of these classes certainly varies from church to church, and teacher to teacher—but all too often there is no clear instructional goal. The Bible is rarely opened. And people go home with little real change in their beliefs or values. Not much real teaching actually takes place.

In terms of training however, things are even more problematic. Because the focus is usually theological, practical skills in evangelism or discipleship are rarely part of the curriculum. Because there is little emphasis on life application, the teaching is often abstract and theological. Because there is no real accountability, few people actually do their Bible studies in advance—much less memorize their assigned verse. And as a result, people can attend for years and never experience any real growth.

This time slot can be used much more effectively. Note these quotes from Counsels on Sabbath School Work (p. 11 & 83):

The Sabbath school should be the place where, through a living connection with God, men and women ... may be so fitted up that they shall be a strength and blessing to the church.

There is much to be done in the Sabbath school work ... in bringing the people to realize their obligation and to act their part. God calls them to work for Him.

Not only is this time slot the ideal time for training, it has the added advantage of keeping the weekdays free for evangelism. Paul's strategy seemed to be to use the sabbath for training, and the weekdays for witnessing. He taught "in the synagogue with the Jews, and with the devout persons [sabbath], and in the market daily [the rest of the week] with them that met with him" (Acts 17:17). If our goal is training workers—we should value trying to keep their week days free for ministry!

To find time for training, simply imitate Paul's example and use the time set apart by God at creation for spiritual growth and development.

Radically Different

Such a class would be radically different from what most members are used to, of course. But we've already explored the core components:

First, it would follow the basic progression outlined earlier. Participants would learn the secrets of internalizing Scripture through effective memorization. They would learn the foundational skills of discipleship: personal prayer, Bible study, obedience, and witnessing. And then they would learn various way to begin reaching out to the people around them in personal ministry. Essentially, each person would be taught how to take in, live out, and pass on God's Word.

Second, it would be modeled on the principles outlined in yesterday's reading. That is, this class would not focus just on the impartation of information, but of skills. There would be practical nuts and bolts suggestions, weekly goals, and regular accountability. Participants would be expected to complete their lesson in advance, and there would be an emphasis on real life application. Each member of the class would eventually be expected to transition into some kind of personal ministry. The class would be laser-focused on training workers.

Granted, not everyone would be drawn to such a class—but there are individuals in every church thirsting for a deeper experience who would be thrilled to be part of something like this. And they would thrive in this kind of environment. And as workers are raised up, your church would begin to grow too. It can happen!

We believe every church should have at least one class committed to this kind of training. And in fact, it may be just about the most important thing we can do:

The greatest help that can be given our people is to teach them to work for God. Christian Service, p 58

Tomorrow we'll look at the subject of motivation, and how to keep your team moving forward...

The Time Problem
Worksheet

How difficult is it today to find time to train believers in the basic skills of discipleship? Why is that?

What are some possible time slots for doing this?

What is the best time to do training, and why? Give several reasons.

What would be the main characteristics of a class specifically designed for training?

Additional Notes:

Maintaining Motivation
Chapter 6

So far we have covered some important concepts: the need to get back to the Great Commission model of making disciples. The stages of growth our curriculum must lead people through. The essential components in a life of true discipleship. The key ingredients in all effective training. And the optimal time slot set apart by God for training workers. These are all critical to launching an effective discipling ministry.

But the mechanics of disciple-making are only part of the solution. The bigger challenge is getting people to commit to training, and then stick to that commitment!

To put it differently (and more precisely), getting started is just 5%, the rest is following through! To establish an effective training ministry, it is important to understand what the Bible teaches about motivation.

Seeing Value

While the word "motivation" is not found in the Bible, Jesus actually told several parables on the subject:

Again, the kingdom of heaven is like unto treasure hid in a field; the which when a man hath found, he hideth, and for joy thereof goeth and selleth all that he hath, and buyeth that field.

Again, the kingdom of heaven is like unto a merchant man, seeking goodly pearls: Who, when he had found one pearl of great price, went and sold all that he had, and bought it. Matthew 13:44-46

In both of these parables, the men clearly demonstrated motivation. Both were highly committed to achieving the object of their desire. And as a result, both of these men were successful in acquiring what they wanted. From this we see that motivation is vital to experiencing a positive outcome. Without it, our training efforts are unlikely to see much success.

Perhaps more important—these parables also show that motivation comes through correctly discerning the value of an object. The first man went and sold all that he had "with joy" for he knew the worth of that treasure hid in the field. Likewise, the merchant eagerly sacrificed all to acquire that one special pearl, for it was "of great price." Neither saw their purchase as a loss, but rather as a gain.

The same is true of training. When a person correctly grasps the value of what they are learning—commitment follows.

The key to keeping a group committed through an extended training program is simply to communicate the value of that training. Encourage them to imagine the impact of having hundreds of verses alive and fresh on the tip of their tongue; the potential of being able to live a life of authentic, practical discipleship; the joys of being able to share their faith with friends consistently, and see at least some come to Christ. Value compels motivation.

On the other hand, should your group lose sight of your training's value—things will quickly degenerate into a string of endless objectives. Team members will lose heart. To persevere, we must constantly encourage those we train to keep their eyes on the prize (Philippians 3:13-14). They must learn to look to the joy set before them (Hebrews 12:2). We must teach them to focus on value. To dwell on the priceless rewards of following Christ.

Count the Cost

Of course, another important truth is also revealed in these parables—that there is a cost for things of value. And there is definitely a cost to training: coming to meetings on time; faithfully completing one's Bible studies in advance; memorizing assigned verses—and quoting them word-perfect; participating in group discussions; carrying out objectives; praying faithfully for fellow team members. All are essential! And they all take self-denial, commitment, and sacrifice.

And our success or failure doesn't only affect us. The Bible is clear about the power of our influence: "exhort one another daily ... lest any of you be hardened through the deceitfulness of sin. For we are made partakers of Christ, if we hold the beginning of our confidence stedfast unto the end" (Hebrews 3:13-14). The prize goes to those who finish—and yet how easy it is to quit just short of the goal! Sin comes in so subtly, and we end up distracted or discouraged. But the solution is clear: exhortation. And apparently, understanding this is going to become increasingly important the closer we get to the end! As Hebrews continues, "consider one another to provoke unto love and to good works ... exhorting one another: and so much the more, as ye see the day approaching" (Hebrews 10:24-25).

To put it differently, each member must understand the power of their influence. Each must recognize their personal responsibility to encourage others in the group, by their example and words. For it is only when each member gives their best to the team—and challenges others to give their best as well, that the group will realize its full potential. They must press toward the goal—together.

A lack of motivation, will lead to half-hearted efforts in your team, and in time, that lack of resolve will spread and weaken the commitment of others in the group as well. A high level of motivation, in contrast, will inspire each group members to strive for excellence. They will all enthusiastically spur each other on to success. A team rises or falls together.

This is part of what it means to count the cost. Before joining a training program, we must challenge each person to honestly evaluate their commitment. "For which of you, intending to build a tower, sitteth not down first, and counteth the cost, whether he have sufficient to finish it?" (Luke 14:28). Motivation involves weighing both cost and value, and then choosing to pay the price.

That's the bottom line, isn't it? Is it really worth it To become a worker? To learn how to multiply? If we are serious about finishing the work, the answer has to be yes.

Tomorrow we look at one more critical key: the secret to real power in your training...

Maintaining Motivation
Discussion Questions

Does the Bible talk about motivation? If so where?

How important is motivation to achieving success?

According to the parables Jesus told, what inspires motivation?

What must we do to ensure ongoing motivation in those we train?

What happens in a training environment when motivation lapses?

What does it mean to count the cost?

What does the Bible say about the power of influence in a training team?

Additional Notes:

An Endtime Urgency
Chapter 7

We've covered a lot of important ground in the preceding pages: the centrality of the Word, the four stages of growth, the key components of discipleship, the training formula, how to maintain motivation, and more. And that's certainly enough to give you a good start in your ministry of disciple-making. I've taught these principles in churches around the world, and wherever they are implemented faithfully, it produces real results.

But I would be remiss to stop here.

In reflecting back over nearly three decades of full time ministry, I can't help but see one more critical concept. In fact, it has only become increasingly important as time has progressed. It's what I call an endtime urgency.

You see, urgency is needed to overcome man's natural lethargy when it comes to spiritual growth. To spark this whole training process. And that urgency flows from a strong sense that the headlines filling the news these days, point to a world spiraling out of control. To a world that's racing toward its final crisis. The crisis predicted in Revelation to immediately precede the return of Christ. A time of great test to the people of God.

And this acceleration of unfolding prophecy implies a call to seek revival, more earnestly, and more urgently than ever before.

A revival of true godliness among us is the greatest and most urgent of all our needs. True Revival, p 9.

For this reason, I believe our training must focus its outcome on equipping men and women to seek revival.

Biblical Revival

The Bible describes the natural man as being in a rather desperate situation. "There is none righteous, no, not one: there is none that understandeth, there is none that seeketh after God. There are all gone out of the way" (Romans 3:10-12). Unfortunately among believers, the situation is often not much better. Revelation describes God's endtime people in particular, as "wretched, and miserable, and poor, and blind, and naked" (Revelation 3:17). Despite all our modern day blessings and advantages, our most pressing problem seems to be how little we grasp our actual condition.

Paul encouraged the believers in his day to fight against spiritual lethargy too. To the Ephesians, he wrote "awake thou that sleepest, and arise from the dead, and Christ shall give thee light" (Ephesians 5:14). He continued his letter to them by exhorting them to walk wisely, to use their time well, to know God's will clearly, and to be filled with the Spirit (Ephesians 5:15-18). These are all blessings that come to us in times of spiritual awakening. In times of revival.

In another place, Paul urged them seek this experience with no delay. "It is high time to awake out of sleep: for now is our salvation nearer than when we believed. The night is far spent, the day is at hand: let us therefore cast off the works of darkness, and let us put on the armour of light" (Romans 13:11-12). If Paul encouraged a sense of urgency then, what would he say to us living today? Especially given the events in our world?

God certainly promises a special awakening among those alive at the end of earth's history. Through the prophet Joel, God promises to pour out His Spirit upon all flesh—men and women, young and old alike (Joel 2:28-29). Through Isaiah, He announces a time when the church will arise and shine, because great light has come. Revelation depicts this revival as a mighty angel coming down from heaven, "having great power; and the earth was lightened with his glory" (Revelation 18:1).

We use terms like the latter rain, the loud cry, the time of refreshing, and others, to describe this great final outpouring of the Spirit, but one thing is for sure—it's going to happen.

The great work of the gospel is not to close with less manifestation of the power of God than marked its opening. (Great Controversy, p 611)

My conclusion in light of all this, is simply that our need for more of the Holy Spirit is more pressing now than ever before. And that the training we offer, needs to be specifically focused on preparing a people to enter into a broader revival experience. That our priority must be to raise up and deploy true revival agents...

Quicken Thou Me

I don't profess to be an expert on future events, but I have seen outpourings of the Holy Spirit personally on a number of occasions, and have been studying the topic of revival for decades. And I have gleaned at least a few insight relevant to training.

First and foremost, revival needs to be rooted in the internalized Word. Revivals linked primarily to a guest speaker, a praise team, or some retreat location, inevitably fizzle out and fade away. What we need is a revival that is linked to something far more powerful, and more enduring. Something we can keep with us wherever we go. I've personally found the Bible to be that exact source of power. As the Psalmist prays, "quicken [revive] thou me according to thy word" (Psalms 119:25). And again, "I will never forget thy precepts: for with them thou hast quickened [revived] me" (Psalms 119:93). Yes, there is power in the Word of God, and I have seen it countless times. Get a person serious about memorizing, and the Word inevitably bursts into life, sparking a deeper experience.

But to strengthen that flame, and keep it burning bright, real discipleship is needed. Deep study of the Word will unlock profound insights that feed our renewed experience. Earnest prayer helps you to identify and remove obstacles to revival in our heart. Diligent obedience opens the way for the Spirit of God to fill our daily life. Just as personal outreach opens the way for the Spirit to fill our ministry. Each of the discipleship components we have studied so far, reinforces and confirms revival. If we want a revival marked by deep earnestness and principled godliness, rather than mere emotionalism and sensationalism, the secret is to keep it rooted in biblical discipleship.

And last but not least, we need to provide specific training in what the Bible teaches about revival itself. How to seek revival, how to spark it, how to sustain it, and how to spread it to others in our church and community. That's the definition of a revival agent, in my mind. One who understands the principles that govern how and when God sends spiritual power to His workers, and who is able to cooperate with God in preparing the way for just such an outpouring. One who seeks that blessing, again and again and again. Until we all transition into that final revival foretold in the Bible, and it is in full force at last.

There is nothing that Satan fears so much as that the people of God shall clear the way by removing every hindrance, so that the Lord can pour out His Spirit ... When the way is prepared for the Spirit of God, the blessing will come. True Revival, p 12.

I believe God is looking for this kind of worker today. And that we have a duty to offer this kind of training to every member in every church. We are too late in prophetic history, to aim for anything less, than a genuine outpouring of endtime spiritual blessings.

Unsurprisingly, this is precisely how we have designed our core curriculum at FAST. Our three step training track boils down to sparking revival through the internalized Word (Survival Kit), strengthening revival through practical discipleship (Basic Training), and spreading revival by equipping revival agents for ministry (Revival Keys). It's the exact process we've talked about before: take it in, live it out, pass it on. But we're going a little further here. We're talking about intentionally focusing every facet of our training on one key goal: revival.

Disciple-making today, must be marked by an endtime urgency. And it must be energized by the power of the Holy Spirit. Time is too short to postpone our need to "arise from the dead", to "awake out of sleep", to "arise and shine". And times are too difficult to attempt the work of disciple-making without an outpouring of the Holy Spirit.

An endtime urgency is vital. Add this focus on revival to your disciple-making toolbox.

An Endtime Urgency
Discussion Questions

Why is urgency needed in the work of making disciples?

How do endtime events inspire a sense of urgency?

What should be our focus in these difficult times given that God promises a special final revival?

What role does each of the following play in the process of preparing for an outpouring of the Holy Spirit:

Bible Memorization

Practical Discipleship

Revival Training

Summarize in your own words, what it means to work as a revival agent:

Additional Notes:

The Missing Key
Chapter 8

In New Testament times, the early church raised up key men and women who scattered throughout the ancient world planting new churches and then transforming those churches into training centers. From these centers streamed out countless men and women preaching the Gospel in every nook and cranny of the Roman Empire. As a result of this explosive combination of evangelism and training, Christ was preached "in all the world" (Colossians 1:6). They finished the work in their generation.

What will it take to finish the work today? Nothing less. Key men and women, scattered throughout our modern world transforming churches into training centers. Training centers able to mobilize members for ministry, and then send them out into every nook and cranny of their communities. When evangelism and training are combined, once again, explosive growth will happen. Revival will break out, the Gospel will go to the world, and the work will be finished—at last.

The Missing Key

Only one thing is needed: "key" men and women to start this process. Individuals who are willing and able to "unlock" their churches and get the process started. They may not end up being the primary teacher or trainer. God may have others in mind for that. But they are the ones who catch the vision, and communicate it to local church leaders. They are the ones who see the potential of their church becoming a true training center. And they are able to communicate the value of that.

God may be calling you to this exact work...

After all, you now know the fundamentals. You know that the best way to begin transforming your church into a training center is to establish a special class for the purpose of training. You know the various stages of growth that training process must cover: Spiritual babes must learn to take in God's Word. Disciples must learn to live it out practically. And workers must learn to share it consistently. You know the essential components of discipleship: Bible study, prayer, personal obedience, and witnessing. And you know how to train: tell them why, show them how, get them started, and keep them going. That your goal is to impart skills, and not just information. You know when and where to do your training. And you know how to build and maintain commitment—by continually emphasizing the value of Bible-based training. And if you do it right, with enough endtime urgency, you know it can lead to great revival in your church. And ultimately to the finishing of the Great commission.

You may not feel like an expert—but you have all the essentials in place, right now.

Training Centers

All you really need are some tools. That's where FAST comes in. In fact, that's our exact mission: to provide cutting-edge tools for men and women who are serious about revitalizing their church (Matthew 28:19-20). Disciple making is no easy task—but we've worked for nearly 30 years to take these principles we've examined and build them into a turn-key curriculum that's easy to use. A curriculum that is proven effective in the lives of thousands. It's tried and true, and it can work for you too!

To begin the process of transforming your church into a training center, simply following these steps:

1) Share this information with your pastor and/or other leaders in your church. Inspire them with the potential of your church becoming a training center, and outline the keys to making that happen.

2) Encourage your church to register as a training center. Registering gives every member access to our complete library of training resources. If your church is unable to do it, gather a few friends, and sponsor your church together, as a group.

3) Start exploring the resources available through your training center. Pick any class that fits with the current needs of your church and begin sharing the appropriate bulletin inserts. With a little effort, you can start getting members here and there to plug in.

4) In particular, explore our training track in personal discipleship. This curriculum gives week by week study guides, and detailed teacher instructions through the whole core discipleship process. You'll find everything you need to go from start to finish. It's a turn-key program you can start running in the lesson study period of your church immediately.

5) Which is the next step: launch your training team. Secure approval to start a small group on our discipleship track. Don't worry if your first group is small—just be faithful in working through the curriculum. There will soon be additional leaders to help train even more. For detailed instructions on how to do lead your team, grab our free Leaders Manual.

6) Repeat. Keep urging training resources and running training teams based on the size and interest level in your church. Be patient, and watch God work.

If you follow these steps, you will soon see a growing band of workers in your church, filled with the memorized Word. Down to business in their personal discipleship. Committed to reaching their community in ministry, and equipped with the skills to do it. And through these key men and women, others will be raised up and trained, who can go on to train even more. All focused on seeking more of the Holy Spirit. On seeking revival.

The explosion will have begun...

Finishing the Work

If you are like me, your heart burns within you at the thought of God's Word going to the ends of the earth in this generation. Because that means Jesus can come at last, and bring all the suffering and pain in this world to an end.

But the Bible makes clear finishing the work will require more workers! According to Jesus, "The harvest truly is plenteous, but the labourers are few" (Matthew 9:37). And in fact, "the work of God in this earth can never be finished until the men and women comprising our church membership rally to the work" (Christian Service, p. 68). Every available Christian must be mobilized.

And God's plan to mobilize all these workers? It's to see every church become a training center. Filled with leaders who understand the stages of growth, the essential spokes of discipleship, the key components of training, the optimal time for training, the secrets of motivation, and our urgent need for revival. All things you know now yourself.

But more than any of these, it starts with just one man or woman—one key person who catches the vision. Someone willing to work to unlock their church as a training center.

Is that missing key you?

The Missing Key
Discussion Questions

What is the one missing "key" needed to "unlock" a church to return to the New Testament model of training centers.

What must these "keys" be able to do?

In what ways can FAST help you in this process?

What are the basic steps involved in creating a training center:

1)

2)

3)

4)

5)

6)

Ultimately, what will it take to finish the work?

What does that imply our strategy should be going forward?

Additional Notes:

FAST Missions
Cutting-Edge Tools and Training

Ready to become a Revival Agent? FAST Missions can help! Our comprehensive training curriculum will give you the skills you need to take in God's Word effectively, live it out practically, and pass it on to others consistently.

Eager to start memorizing God's Word? Our powerful keys will transform your ability to hide Scripture in your heart.

Want to explore the secrets of "real life" discipleship? Our next level training zooms in on critical keys to growth, like Bible study, prayer, time management, and more.

Want to become a worker in the cause of Christ? Our most advanced training is designed to give you the exact ministry skills you need to see revival spread.

For more information, please visit us at:
WWW.FASTMISSIONS.COM

Study Guides

Looking for life-changing study guides to use in your small group or Bible study class? These resources have been used by thousands around the world. You could be next!

Survival Kit
Want to learn how to memorize Scripture effectively? These study guides will teach you 10 keys to memorization, all drawn straight from the Bible. Our most popular course ever!

Basic Training
Discover nuts and bolts keys to the core skills of discipleship: prayer, Bible study, time management, and more. Then learn how to share these skills with others. It is the course that launched our ministry!

Revival Keys
Now as never before, God's people need revival. And these guides can show you how to spark revival in your family, church, and community. A great revival is coming. Are you ready?

Online Classes

Want to try out some of the resources available at FAST? Here is just a small sampling of courses from among dozens of personal and small group study resources:

Crash Course
Discover Bible-based keys to effective memorization.
http://fast.st/cc

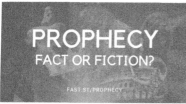

Fact or Fiction
Does the Bible really predict future events? You be the judge.
http://fast.st/prophecy

Monkey Business
Find out how evolution flunks the science test.
http://fast.st/monkey

Dry Bones
Want more of God's Spirit? Learn how to pursue revival.
http://fast.st/bones

The Lost Art
Rediscover New Testament keys to making disciples.
http://fast.st/lostart

Digital Tools

FAST offers a number of powerful "apps for the soul" you can use to grow in your walk with God. And many of these are completely free to anyone with an account. Some of these include:

Memory Engine
Our powerful review engine is designed to help ensure effective longterm Bible memorization. Give it a try, it works!

Bible Reading
An innovative Bible reading tool to help you read through the entire Bible, at your own pace, and in any order you want.

Prayer Journal
Use this tool to organize important requests, and we'll remind you to pray for them on the schedule you want.

Time Management
Learn how to be more productive, by keeping track of what you need to do and when. Just log in daily and get stuff done.

For more information about more than twenty tools like these, please visit us at *http://fast.st/tools.*

Books

If the content of this little book stirred your heart, look for these titles by the same author.

For Such A Time...
A challenging look at the importance of memorization for the last days, including topics such as the Three Angel's messages and the Latter Rain.

Moral Machinery
Discover how our spiritual, mental, and physical faculties work together using the sanctuary as a blueprint. Astonishing insights that could revolutionize your life!

The Movement
Discover God's plan to finish the work through a powerful endtime movement. Gain critical insights into what lies just ahead for the remnant!

Made in the USA
Middletown, DE
17 June 2022

67188405R00040